ESSENTIAL CHINESE CHARACTERS

CHINESE WRITING FOR KIDS

WORKBOOK **2** CHARACTERS 101-200

LingLing

www.linglingmandarin.com

Copyright © 2025 Ling He (LingLing Mandarin)

All rights reserved. No part of this book including audio material may be reproduced or used in any manner without written permission of the copyright owner. For more information, contact:

enquiries@linglingmandarin.com

FIRST EDITION

Editing by Xinrong Huo
Cover design by LingLing

www.linglingmandarin.com

CONTENTS

INTRODUCTION 5
Welcome 5
Radicals And Character Composition 5
Learning Chinese Is Fun 5
What's In The Book 6
Learn, Practice, Have Fun 6

CHINESE STROKES 7
Basic Strokes 7
Basic Writing Rules 9

CHARACTER COMPOSITION 10
How Chinese Characters Are Formed 10

CHINESE RADICALS 14
Learning More Radicals 14
Writing Practice 15

CHINESE CHARACTERS 23
Your Next 100 Chinese Characters 23

	Universe	日月星云天地	24
	Natural Elements	山海江河水火金石土田	27
	Plants	木树花草	32
	Shapes And Forms	方圆胖瘦深浅	34
	Communications	听说读写画看问吵	37
	Actions	坐起开关进出做停飞游走跑动爬唱跳打骑	41
	Animals	鼠牛虎兔龙蛇马羊猴鸡狗猪猫虫鱼鸟	50
	Colors	红橙黄绿蓝紫粉棕白黑	58
	Furniture	桌椅床柜	63
	Condition And Appearance	美丑老幼新旧干湿	65
	Quality And State	好坏快慢重轻香臭忙闲	69

RESOURCES 74
Access Audio 74
300 Essential Chinese Characters Workbook Series 74
Writing Practice Books 75
Beginner Books 75

Character	Pinyin	English	Page
日	rì	the sun; day	24
月	yuè	the moon	24
星	xīng	star	25
云	yún	cloud	25
天	tiān	heaven; sky	26
地	dì	earth; ground	26
山	shān	mountain	27
海	hǎi	sea	27
江	jiāng	river (wide & long)	28
河	hé	river (narrow)	28
水	shuǐ	water	29
火	huǒ	fire	29
金	jīn	gold	30
石	shí	stone	30
土	tǔ	soil; dirt	31
田	tián	farm; field	31
木	mù	wood	32
树	shù	tree	32
花	huā	flower	33
草	cǎo	grass	33
方	fāng	square	34
圆	yuán	round; circle	34
胖	pàng	fat	35
瘦	shòu	slim; thin	35
深	shēn	deep	36
浅	qiǎn	shallow	36
听	tīng	to listen	37
说	shuō	to talk	37
读	dú	to read	38
写	xiě	to write	38
画	huà	to draw	39
看	kàn	to look; to read	39
问	wèn	to ask	40
吵	chǎo	to quarrel	40
坐	zuò	to sit	41
起	qǐ	to rise	41
开	kāi	to open; turn on	42
关	guān	to close; turn off	42
进	jìn	to enter	43
出	chū	to go out	43
做	zuò	to do	44
停	tíng	to stop	44
飞	fēi	to fly	45
游	yóu	to swim	45
走	zǒu	to walk	46
跑	pǎo	to run	46
动	dòng	to move	47
爬	pá	to climb	47
唱	chàng	to sing	48
跳	tiào	to jump; dance	48

Character	Pinyin	English	Page
打	dǎ	to hit; to beat	49
骑	qí	to ride	49
鼠	shǔ	mouse; rat	50
牛	niú	cow; ox	50
虎	hǔ	tiger	51
兔	tù	rabbit	51
龙	lóng	dragon	52
蛇	shé	snake	52
马	mǎ	horse	53
羊	yáng	sheep; goat	53
猴	hóu	monkey	54
鸡	jī	chicken; rooster	54
狗	gǒu	dog	55
猪	zhū	pig	55
猫	māo	cat	56
虫	chóng	insect; worm	56
鱼	yú	fish	57
鸟	niǎo	bird	57
红	hóng	red	58
橙	chéng	orange	58
黄	huáng	yellow	59
绿	lǜ	green	59
蓝	lán	blue	60
紫	zǐ	purple	60
粉	fěn	pink; powder	61
棕	zōng	brown	61
白	bái	white	62
黑	hēi	black	62
桌	zhuō	table	63
椅	yǐ	chair	63
床	chuáng	bed	64
柜	guì	cabinet	64
美	měi	beautiful	65
丑	chǒu	ugly	65
老	lǎo	old (age)	66
幼	yòu	little (age)	66
新	xīn	new	67
旧	jiù	old (condition)	67
干	gān	dry	68
湿	shī	wet	68
好	hǎo	good	69
坏	huài	bad	69
快	kuài	fast	70
慢	màn	slow	70
重	zhòng	heavy	71
轻	qīng	light	71
香	xiāng	fragrant	72
臭	chòu	smelly	72
忙	máng	busy	73
闲	xián	idle	73

INTRODUCTION

WELCOME

Welcome back to the **300 Essential Chinese Characters Workbook Series**! This is the second book in the **three-book** series, where you'll reach a new level by learning to write another 100 Chinese characters. Completing this workbook, along with Workbook 1, marks an amazing milestone—200 Chinese characters mastered!

RADICALS AND CHARACTER COMPOSITION

In Workbook 1, you mastered the 60 most common radicals and your first 100 Chinese characters, building a solid foundation for your Chinese writing journey. In this book you'll progress further by studying character composition from 20 examples, mastering 48 additional radicals, and learning 100 new characters.

LEARNING CHINESE IS FUN

Do you remember from the first book that Chinese characters are often pictographic, meaning many look like the objects they represent. This makes learning them feel like solving a puzzle or creating a piece of art.

For example, the character for "moon" (月) looks like a crescent moon hanging in the sky, with its curved shape and lines resembling the moon's soft glow. The character for "fire" (火) resembles flames rising upward, with its strokes spreading out like flickering tongues of fire. The character for "field" (田) resembles farmland, its square shape divided into sections that evoke the neat rows of crops in a cultivated field.

WHAT'S IN THE BOOK

In Chapter 1, you will review Chinese writing rules and the eight basic strokes, then study the rules of character composition and master 48 additional radicals. In Chapter 2, you will learn to write 100 new characters (Simplified Chinese, used in Mainland China), covering everyday topics such as nature and universe, shapes, movements, animals, colors, and more.

Each character includes:

- **Meaning** - What the character represents.
- **Pinyin** - How to pronounce it in Chinese.
- **Radical** - A clue to its meaning.
- **Stroke Order** - The correct way to write it beautifully.
- **Common Words** - Practical examples for everyday use.
- **Color Picture** - An engaging visual aid to help you remember the meaning.
- **FREE Downloadable Audio** - To help with pronunciation - check the **Access Audio** page to download.

With plenty of space to practice, you'll trace each character and refine your skills! Step by step, you'll gain confidence, deepen your understanding, and build a strong foundation for advancing in Chinese. Keep going—you've got this!

LEARN, PRACTICE, HAVE FUN

Learning Chinese is like planting a tree—each character you learn is like a seed that will grow into a tall, strong tree of knowledge. The more you practice, the better you'll get, just like the Chinese idiom:

BASIC STROKES

In the first book, you learnt the basic strokes. Here's a quick reminder of the eight basic Chinese strokes in Chinese writing, often called the "Eight Principles of Yong (永)" because they can be seen in the character 永 (which means "forever"). Learning these eight strokes is important because they are the building blocks for all Chinese characters.

We've included all the information and practice space as in the first book; remember "repetition is the mother of learning," so why not take the opportunity to refresh your memory and practice a little more.

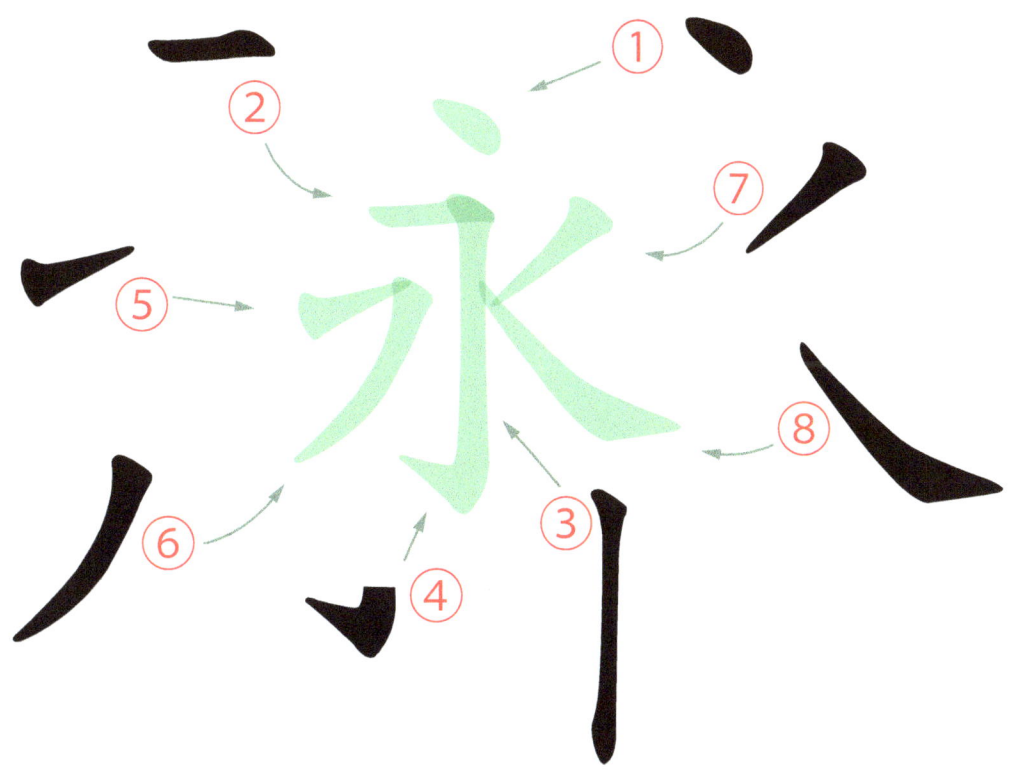

BASIC WRITING RULES

When writing Chinese characters, there are some important rules to follow to ensure proper structure and balance. These rules will help you to write each stroke in the right order and will make writing easier and more straightforward, ensuring your characters remain neat and easy to read. If ever you forget, just come back here to refresh your memory!

Top to Bottom

sky

Left to Right

 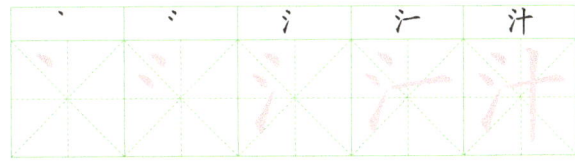

juice

Horizontal, then Vertical

 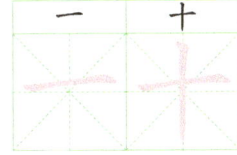

ten

Left-falling, then Right-falling

 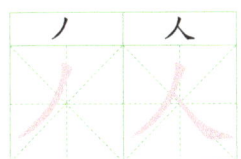

person

Middle then Sides (when symmetrical)

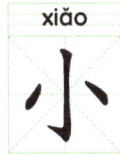 

small

Outside to Inside, then Close

 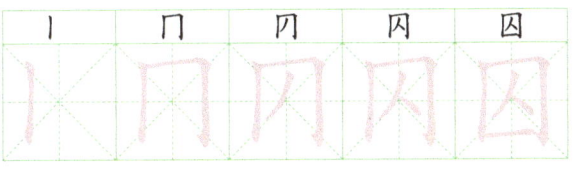

prisoner

CHARACTER COMPOSITION

HOW CHINESE CHARACTERS ARE FORMED

Chinese characters are like fun puzzles, made of smaller pieces called components, each with its own meaning or sound. By combining these components, new characters with different meanings are formed.

In Workbook 1, we introduced the 60 most common radicals, showing how they combine with other components to create characters. Radicals can be smaller parts or independent characters.

For instance, the plant radical 艹 + 化 (to change) = 花 (flower), symbolizing a plant that transforms into a flower.

Or, the sun radical/character 日 + 月 (the moon) = 明 (bright), symbolizing the light of the sun and moon together, representing ultimate brightness and clarity.

By understanding these "building blocks," you can often guess the meaning or pronunciation of unfamiliar characters. Let's take a look at some examples!

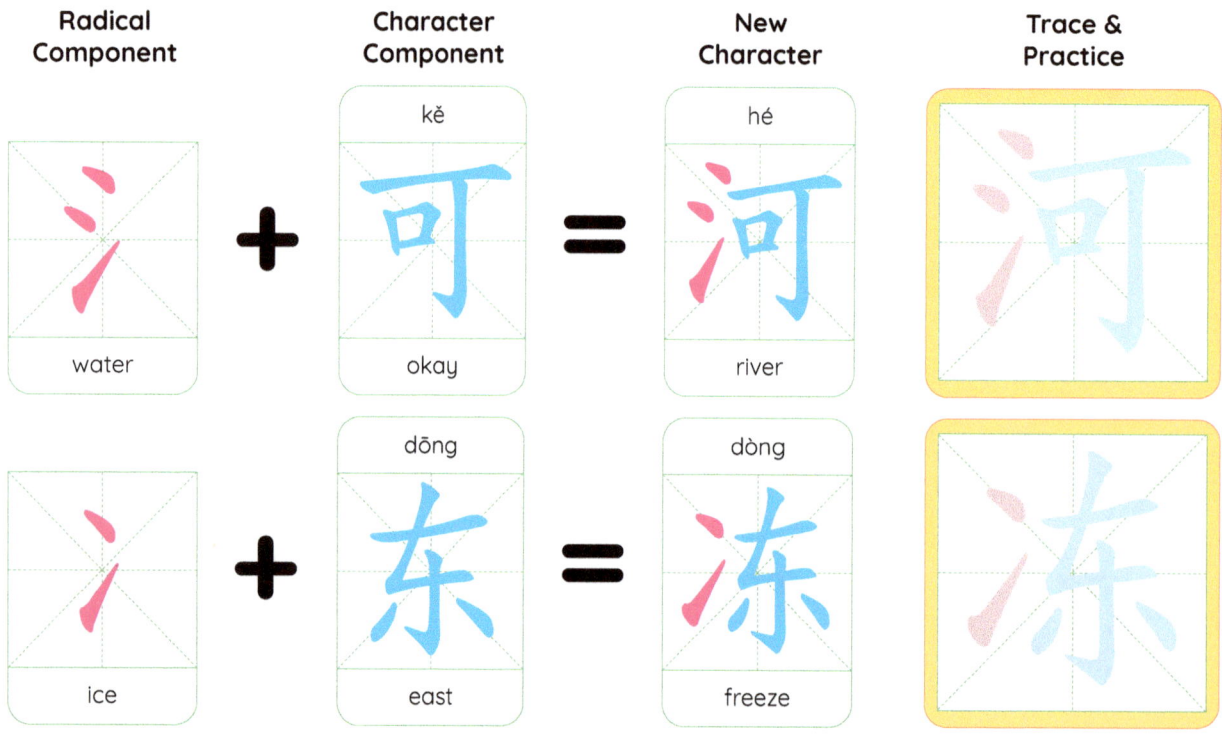

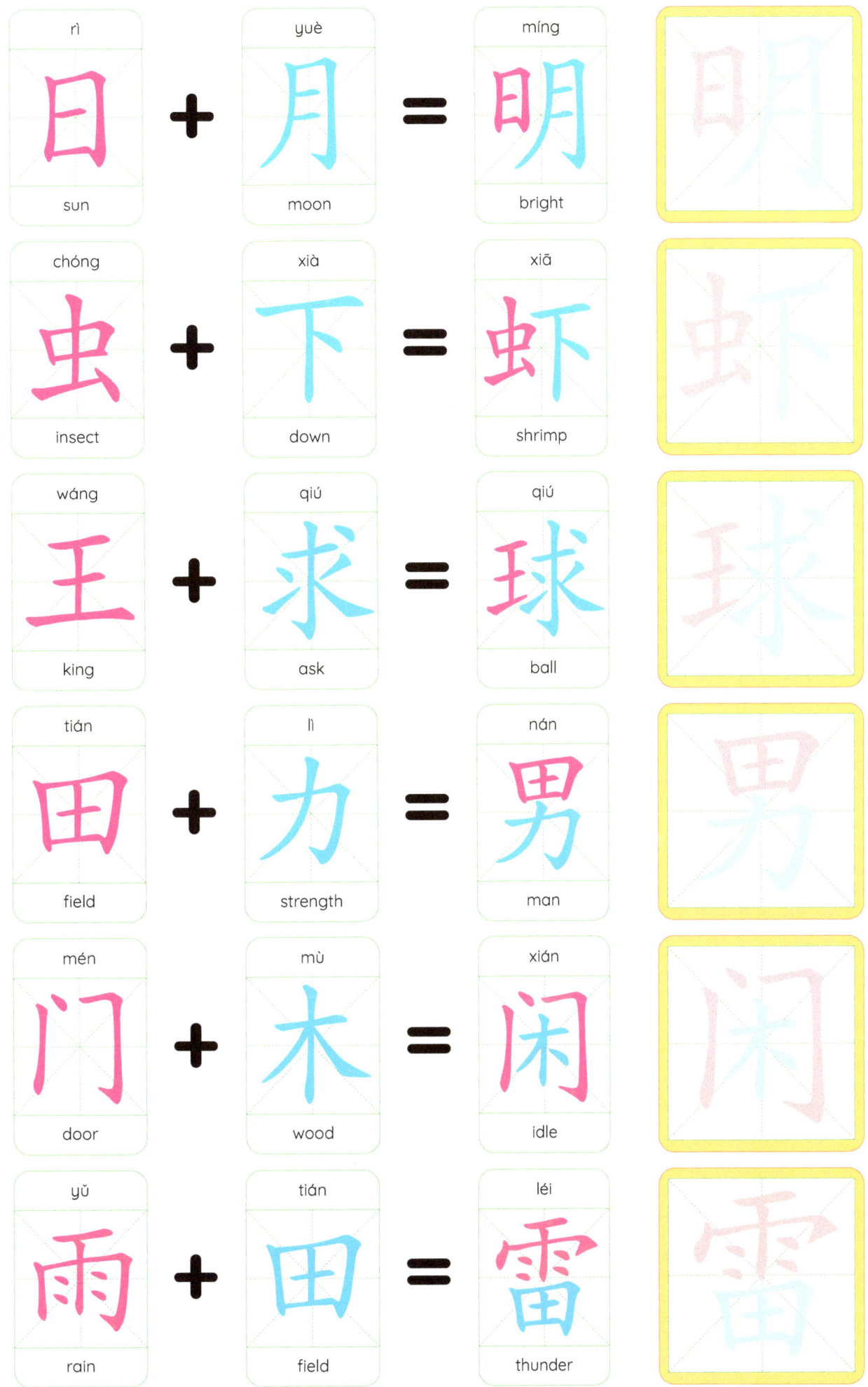

CHINESE RADICALS

LEARNING MORE RADICALS

In Workbook 1, we explored the 60 most common radicals, which are the building blocks of Chinese characters. We gained a deeper understanding of this through the rules of character composition covered in the previous pages, learning that radicals often provide important clues about a character's meaning or how it connects to other characters.

In Workbook 2, we'll build on this strong foundation by introducing 48 more radicals. These new radicals will help you unlock even more characters, giving you tools to better understand their meanings. With every radical you learn, decoding and remembering Chinese characters will become easier and more exciting.

Now, let's practice drawing the radicals! Use the arrows and numbers to learn how to draw each stroke in the correct order and direction. Then for each example simply trace the **radical** (don't worry about drawing the full character in the example for now, we'll practice many of those later). Have fun writing!

A Radical
B Radical Meaning
C Stroke Order
D Stroke Direction
E Example Character
F Character Pinyin
G Character Meaning
H Trace the radical strokes in the example (shown in pink).

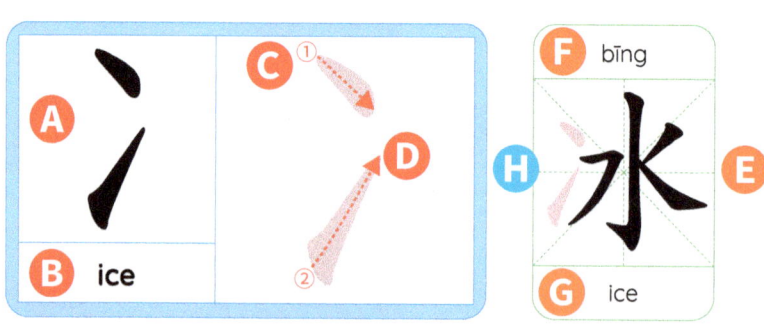

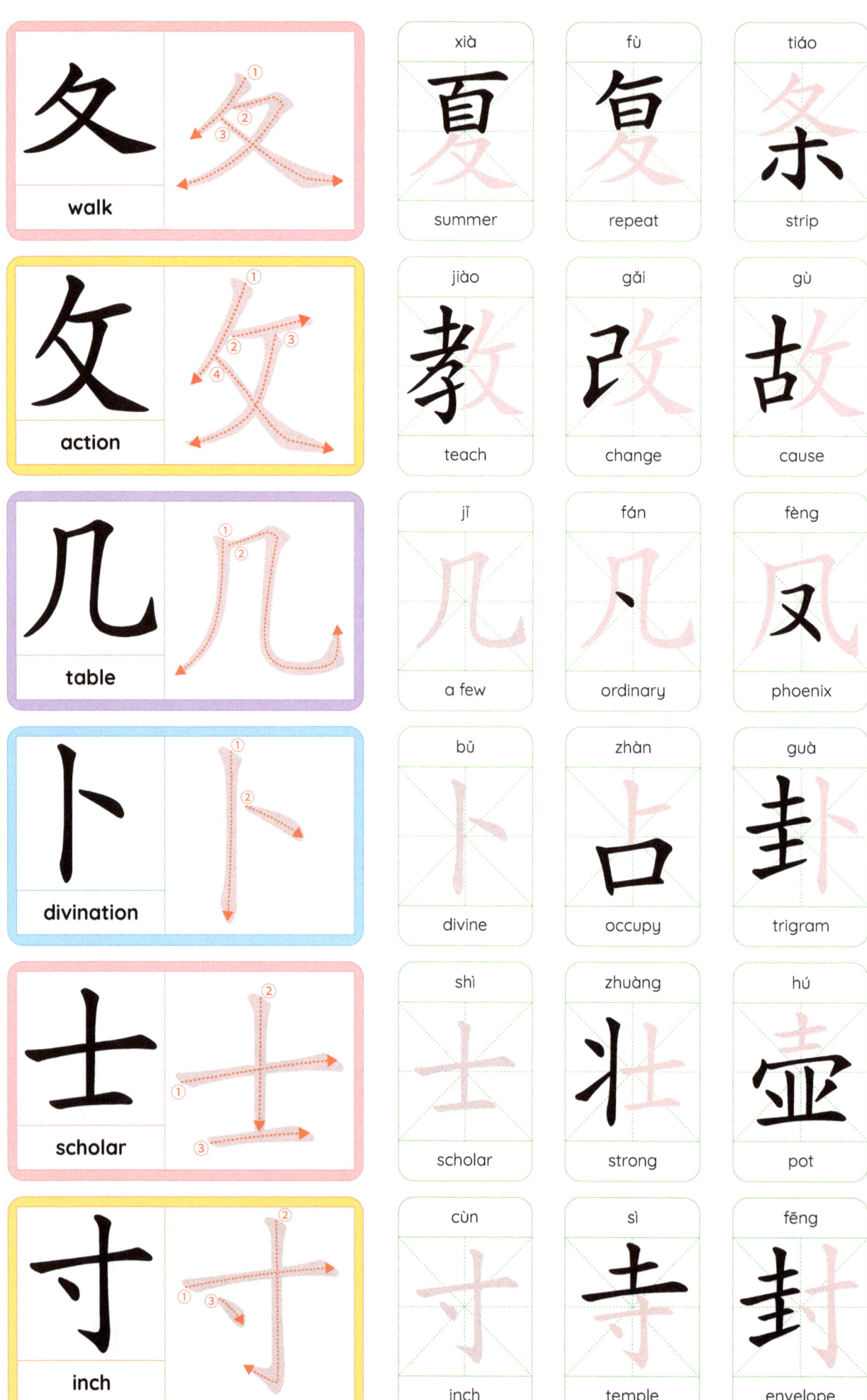

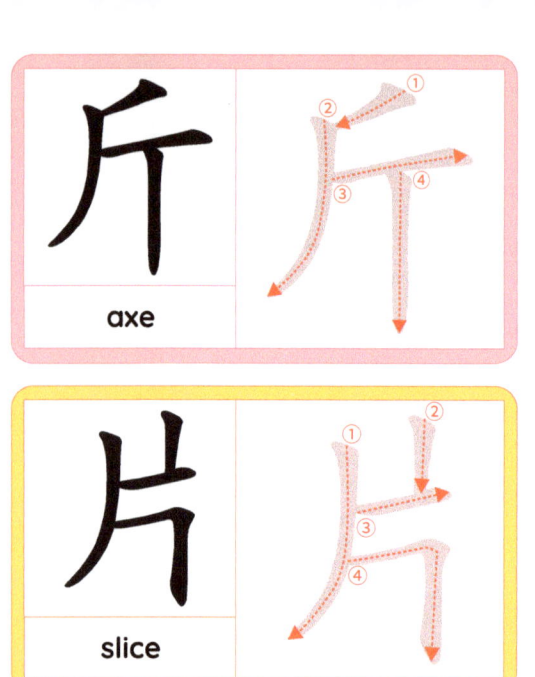
axe

jīn	xīn	duàn
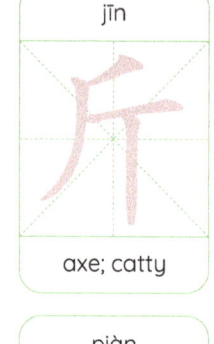		
axe; catty	new	break

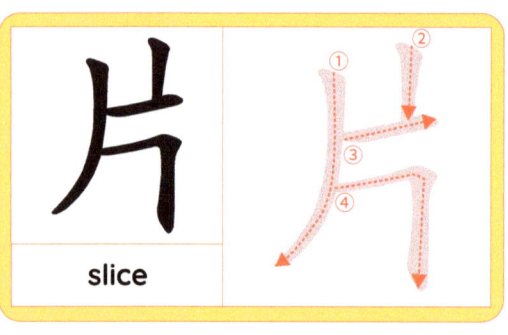
slice

piàn	pái	bǎn
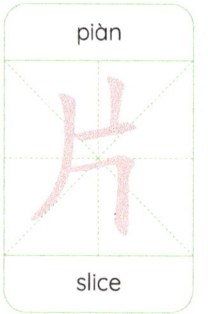		
slice	signboard	edition

tile

wǎ	píng	cí

tile	bottle	porcelain

west

xī	yào	piào
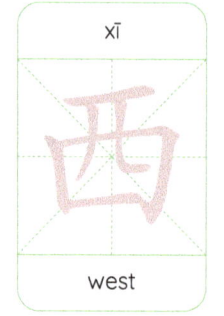		
west	want	ticket

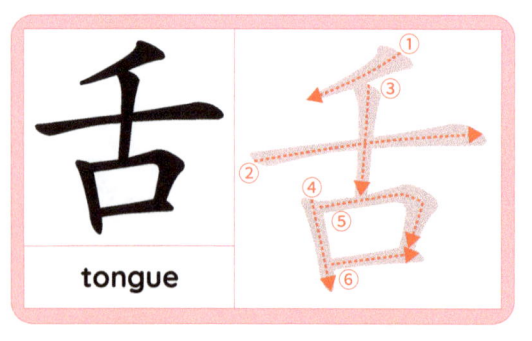
tongue

shé	shě	tiǎn

tongue	abandon	to lick

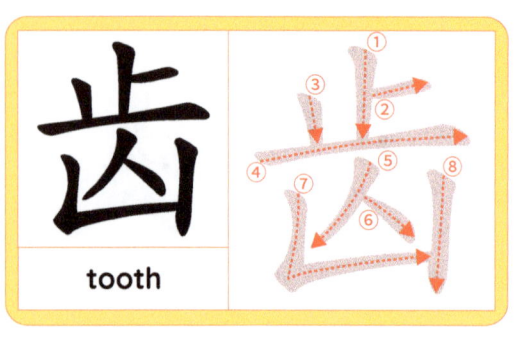
tooth

chǐ	líng	yín

tooth	age	gum

耳 ear	ěr 耳 ear	cōng 聪 clever	liáo 聊 to chat
鱼 fish	yú 鱼 fish	xiān 鲜 fresh	lǔ 鲁 rude
虎 tiger	hǔ 虎 tiger	lǔ 虏 captive	qián 虔 reverent
犬 dog	quǎn 犬 dog (classical)	zhuàng 状 form	xiàn 献 to offer
牛 cow	niú 牛 cow	wù 物 thing	qiān 牵 to pull
龙 dragon	lóng 龙 dragon	gōng 龚 respect	lǒng 垄 monopolize

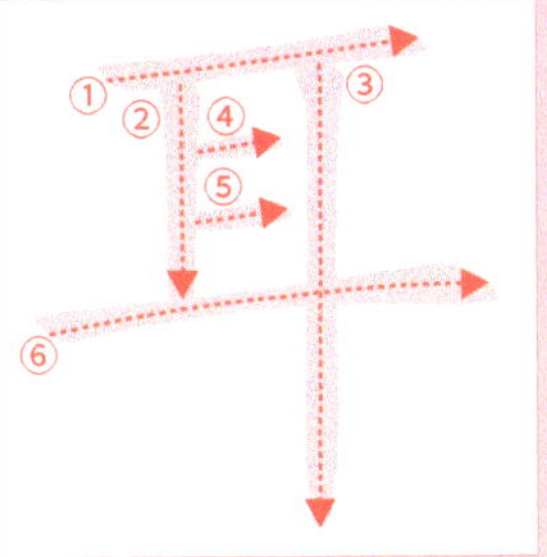

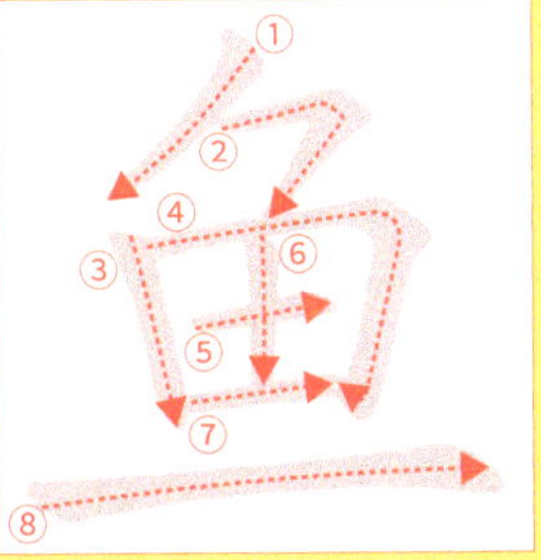

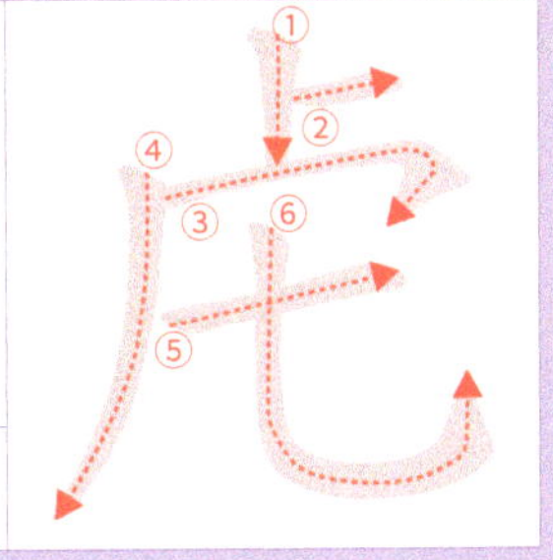

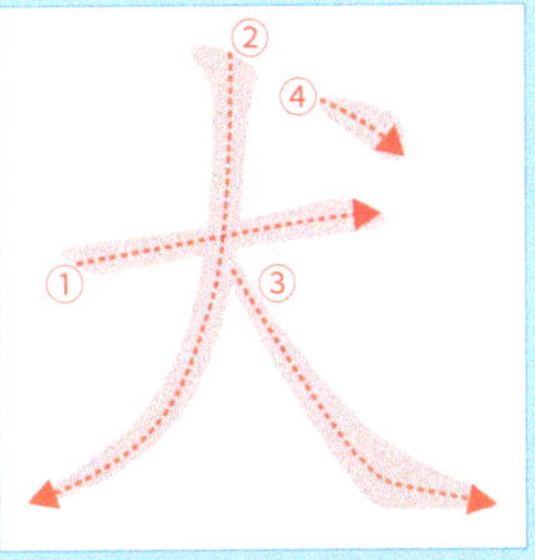

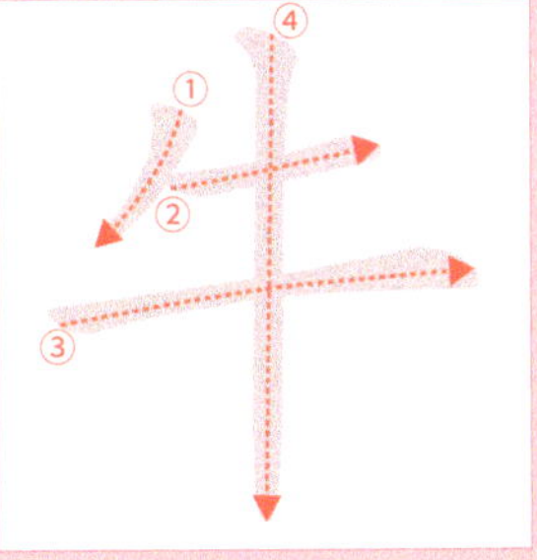

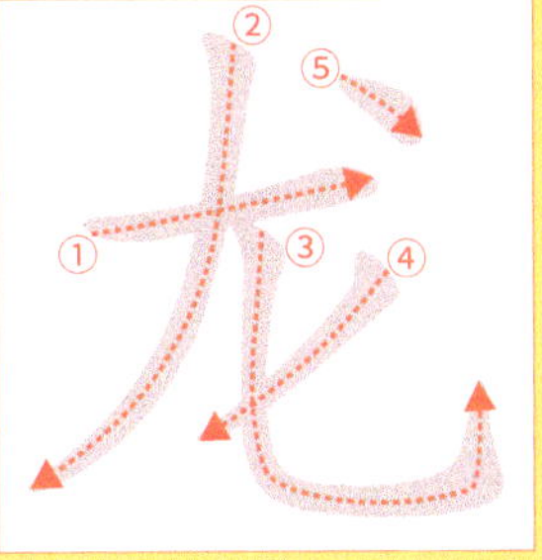

CHINESE CHARACTERS

YOUR NEXT 100 CHINESE CHARACTERS

It's time to take the next step and learn your second set of 100 characters!

Just as in Workbook 1, start by tracing each character to build muscle memory, then challenge yourself to write them on your own. For every character, you'll find three lines to trace and practice writing, and one final line to write freely without tracing. You've got this—I believe in you!

Mistakes are part of the journey, so don't worry if they happen. With practice, your writing will improve, and your confidence will grow. Take your time, don't rush to fill in all the boxes. Don't forget to look at the example words for each character to supercharge your learning! Most importantly, enjoy the process and have fun discovering the art of Chinese characters!

加油!
You can do it!

Need more space to practice?

UNIVERSE

rì
日
the Sun; day

丨 冂 日 日

EXAMPLES

节日	jié rì	festival
日子	rì zi	day (s)
日期	rì qī	date

Radical: 日   Strokes: 4

yuè
月
the Moon

丿 刀 月 月

EXAMPLES

月亮	yuè liang	the moon
月光	yuè guāng	moonlight
月饼	yuè bǐng	mooncake

Radical: 月   Strokes: 4

— 24 —

UNIVERSE

EXAMPLES

星星	xīng xing	star(s)
星期	xīng qī	week
星空	xīng kōng	stary sky

Radical: 日   Strokes: 9

EXAMPLES

多云	duō yún	cloudy
白云	bái yún	white cloud
乌云	wū yún	dark cloud

Radical: 二   Strokes: 4

UNIVERSE

tiān — heaven; sky

一 二 干 天

EXAMPLES

天上	tiān shàng	in the sky
天下	tiān xià	the world
天空	tiān kōng	sky

Radical: 大   Strokes: 4

dì — earth; ground

一 十 土 圠 地 地

EXAMPLES

地上	dì shàng	on the ground
地下	dì xià	underground
地球	dì qiú	the Earth

Radical: 土   Strokes: 6

NATURAL ELEMENTS

EXAMPLES

山上	shān shàng	in the mountain
山下	shān xià	mountain foot
山顶	shān dǐng	mountain peak

Radical: 山　　Strokes: 3

EXAMPLES

大海	dà hǎi	(vast) sea
海洋	hǎi yáng	ocean
海岛	hǎi dǎo	island

Radical: 氵　　Strokes: 10

NATURAL ELEMENTS

EXAMPLES

长江	cháng jiāng	Yangtze River
江山	jiāng shān	landscape (of a country)
江边	jiāng biān	riverside

Radical: 氵   Strokes: 6

EXAMPLES

黄河	huáng hé	Yellow River
河水	hé shuǐ	river water
过河	guò hé	to cross the river

Radical: 氵   Strokes: 8

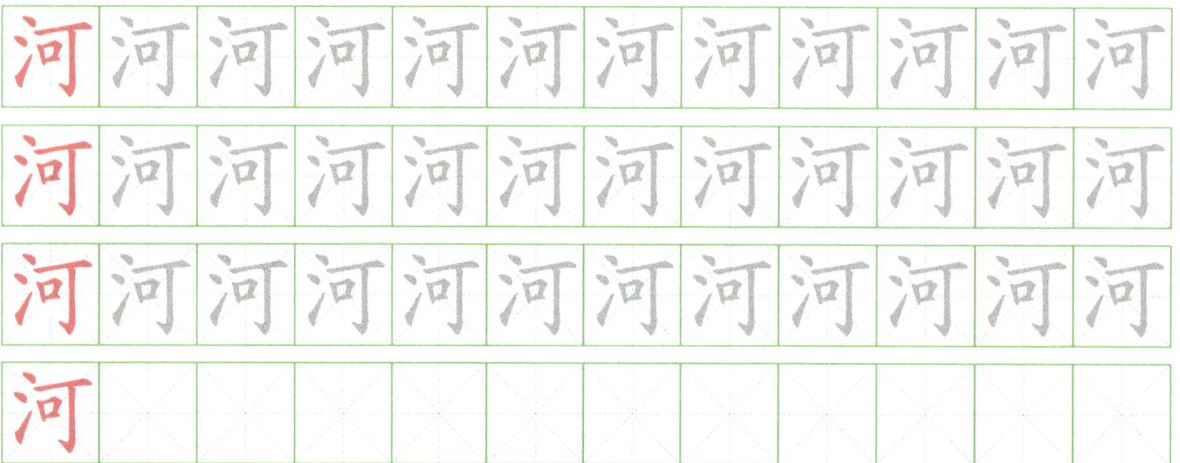

— 28 —

NATURAL ELEMENTS

EXAMPLES

水星	shuǐ xīng	Mercury
水果	shuǐ guǒ	fruit
水流	shuǐ liú	water flow

Radical: 水   Strokes: 4

EXAMPLES

火星	huǒ xīng	Mars
火鸡	huǒ jī	turkey
火车	huǒ chē	train

Radical: 火   Strokes: 4

NATURAL ELEMENTS

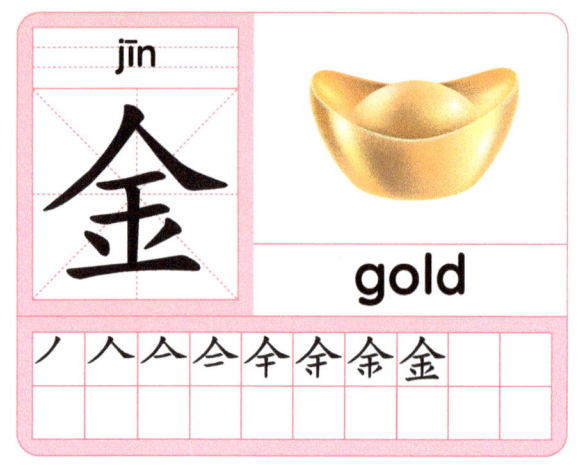

EXAMPLES

金星	jīn xīng	Venus
金子	jīn zi	solid gold
金钱	jīn qián	money

Radical: 金　　Strokes: 8

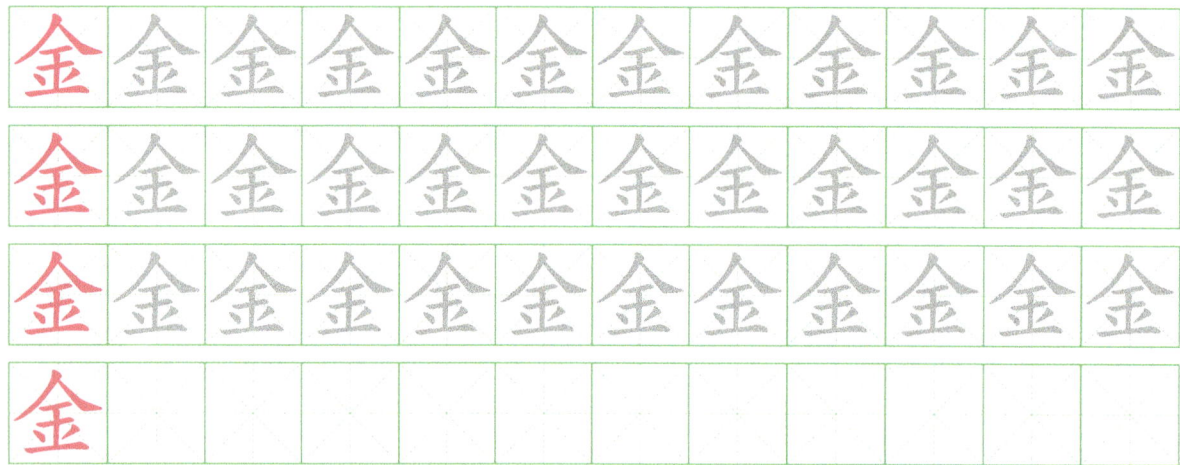

EXAMPLES

石头	shí tou	stone; rock
石门	shí mén	stone gate
石油	shí yóu	oil (petroleum)

Radical: 石　　Strokes: 5

NATURAL ELEMENTS

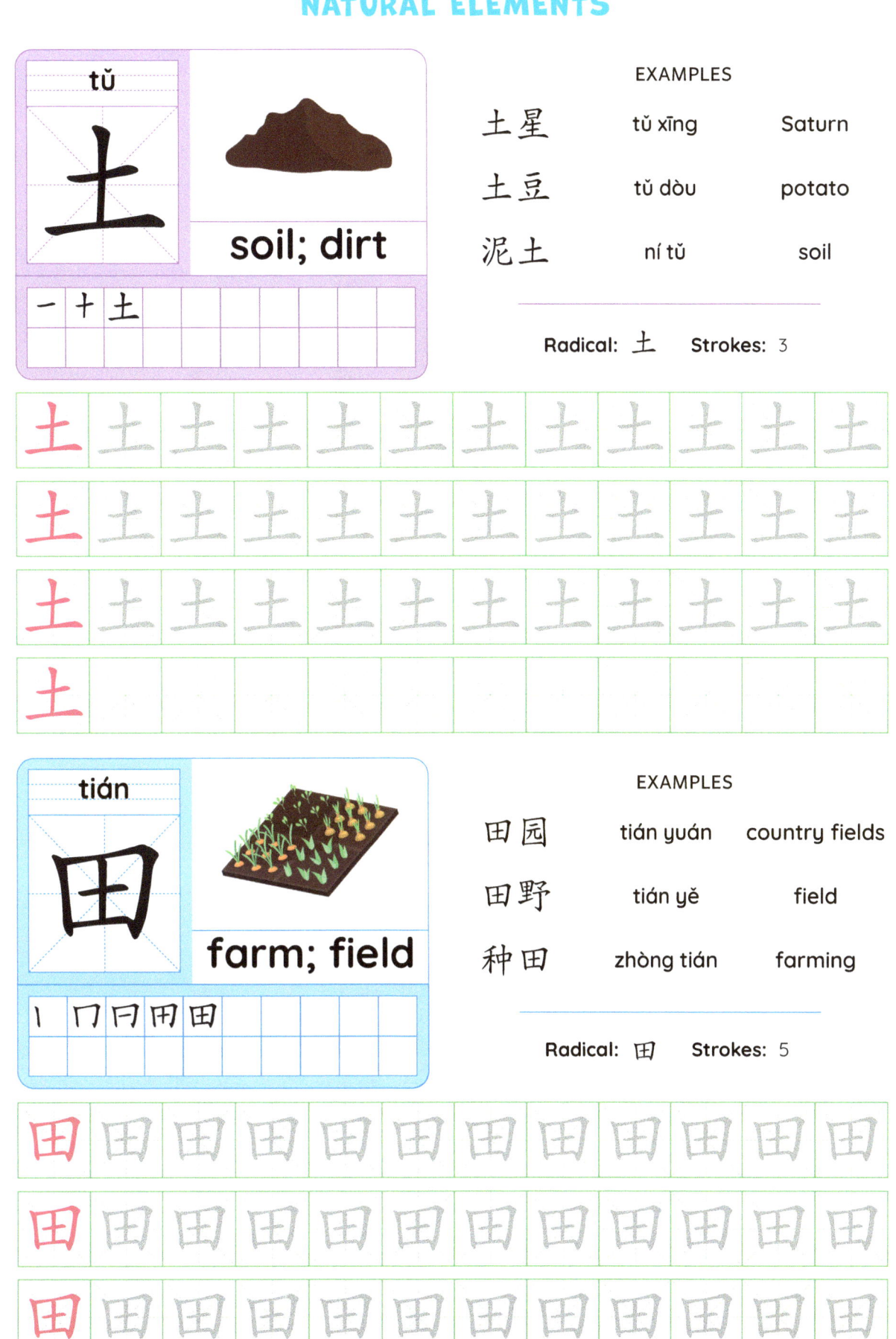

tǔ — soil; dirt

一 十 土

	Examples	
土星	tǔ xīng	Saturn
土豆	tǔ dòu	potato
泥土	ní tǔ	soil

Radical: 土   Strokes: 3

tián — farm; field

丨 冂 日 田 田

	Examples	
田园	tián yuán	country fields
田野	tián yě	field
种田	zhòng tián	farming

Radical: 田   Strokes: 5

PLANTS

EXAMPLES

木星	mù xīng	Jupiter
木头	mù tou	wood
木屋	mù wū	wooden house

Radical: 木   Strokes: 4

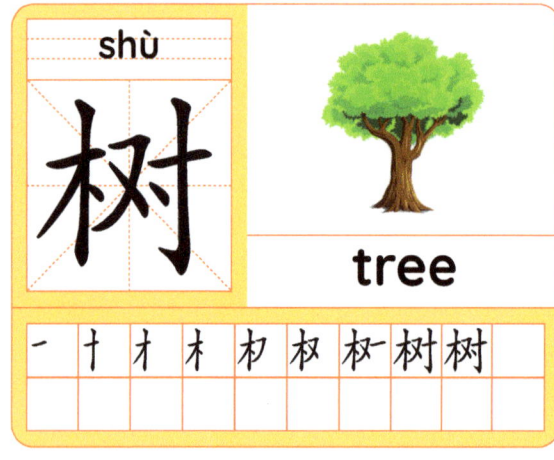

EXAMPLES

大树	dà shù	big tree
树叶	shù yè	leaf
树林	shù lín	woods

Radical: 木   Strokes: 9

PLANTS

huā — flower

一 十 卝 艹 艻 芀 花

雪花	xuě huā	snowflake
桃花	táo huā	peach blossoms
烟花	yān huā	fireworks

Radical: 艹   Strokes: 7

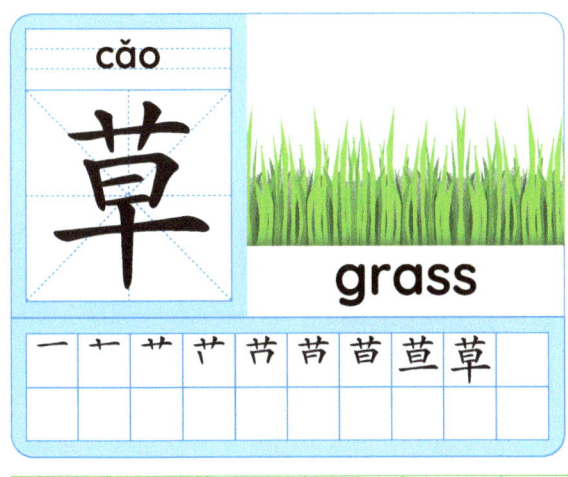

cǎo — grass

一 十 卝 艹 艼 艿 苩 苩 草

小草	xiǎo cǎo	grass (short)
草地	cǎo dì	grassland
草莓	cǎo méi	strawberry

Radical: 艹   Strokes: 9

SHAPES AND FORMS

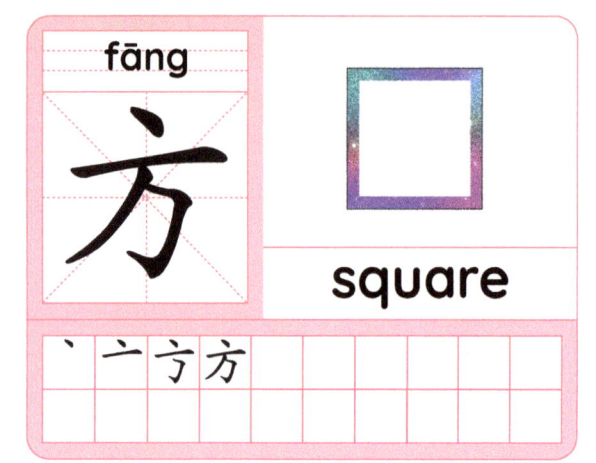

EXAMPLES

方向	fāng xiàng	direction
方法	fāng fǎ	method
方面	fāng miàn	aspect

Radical: 方   Strokes: 4

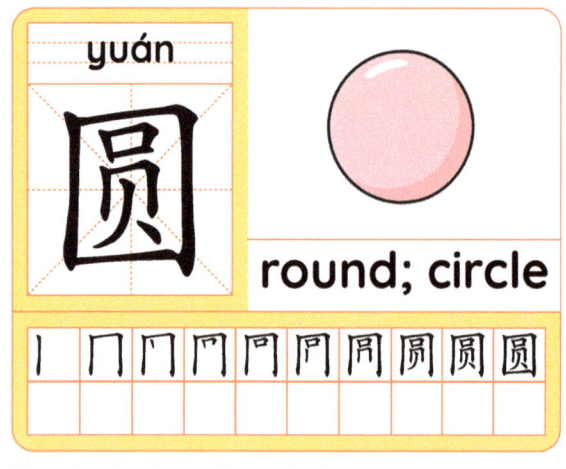

EXAMPLES

圆形	yuán xíng	round shape
圆月	yuán yuè	full moon
圆桌	yuán zhuō	round table

Radical: 囗   Strokes: 10

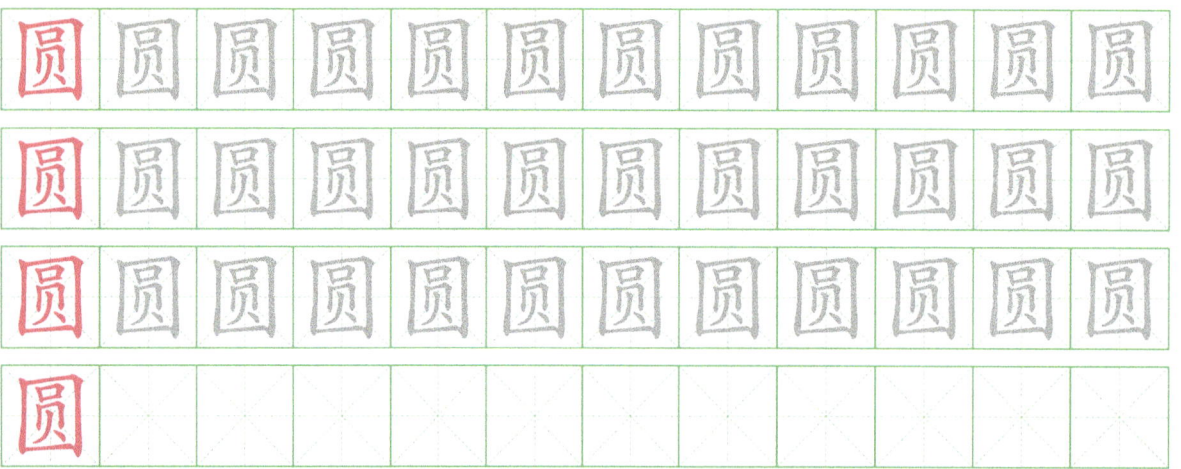

— 34 —

SHAPES AND FORMS

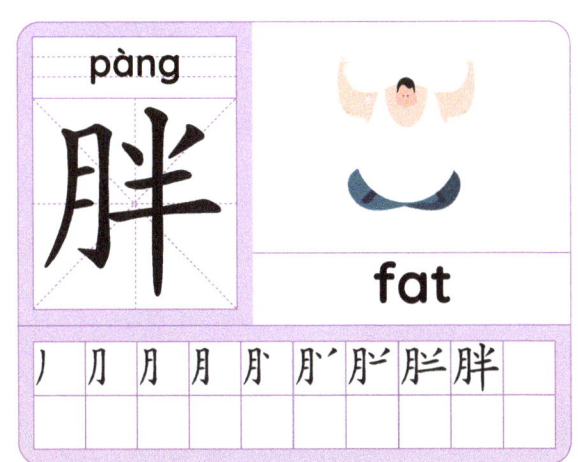

pàng
胖
fat

丿 丿 刀 月 月 月 肝 胖 胖

EXAMPLES

很胖	hěn pàng	very fat
胖子	pàng zi	fat person
不胖	bú pàng	not fat

Radical: 月   Strokes: 9

shòu
瘦
slim; thin

丶 亠 广 广 广 疒 疒 疒 疖 疒 疼 痩 瘦

EXAMPLES

很瘦	hěn shòu	very thin
瘦子	shòu zi	thin person
不瘦	bú shòu	not slim

Radical: 疒   Strokes: 14

— 35 —

SHAPES AND FORMS

shēn 深 — deep

EXAMPLES

很深	hěn shēn	very deep
深色	shēn sè	dark color
深水	shēn shuǐ	deep water

Radical: 氵　Strokes: 11

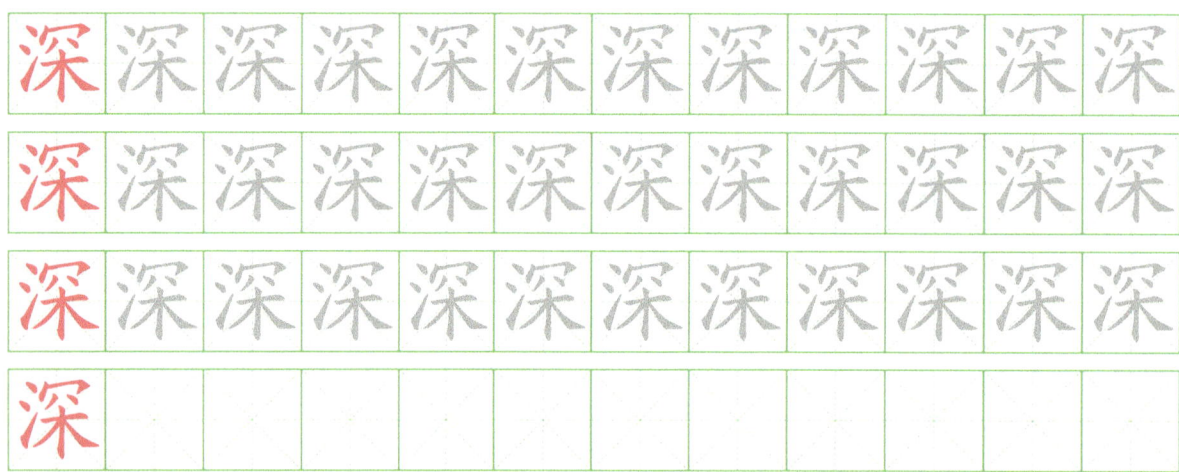

qiǎn 浅 — shallow

EXAMPLES

很浅	hěn qiǎn	very shallow
浅色	qiǎn sè	light color
浅水	qiǎn shuǐ	shallow water

Radical: 氵　Strokes: 8

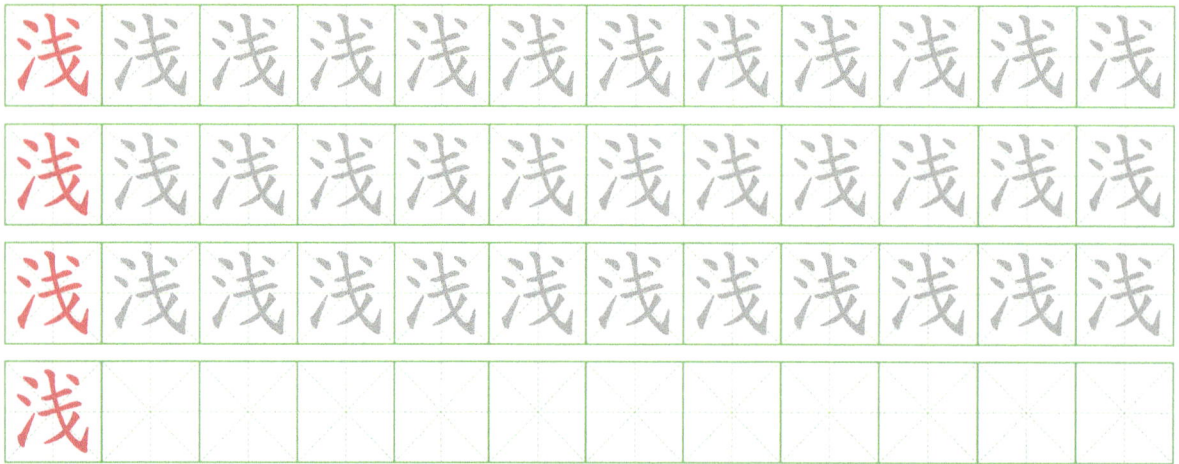

COMMUNICATIONS

EXAMPLES

听话	tīng huà	obedient
听说	tīng shuō	to hear (of)
听音乐	tīng yīn yuè	to listen to music

Radical: 口   Strokes: 7

EXAMPLES

说话	shuō huà	to talk
说明	shuō míng	to indicate
说不说	shuō bu shuō	to talk or not

Radical: 讠   Strokes: 9

COMMUNICATIONS

EXAMPLES

读书	dú shū	to read books (aloud)
读者	dú zhě	reader
读不读	dú bu dú	to read or not

Radical: 讠　　Strokes: 10

EXAMPLES

写字	xiě zì	to write
写信	xiě xìn	to write letters
写错	xiě cuò	to write incorrectly

Radical: 冖　　Strokes: 5

COMMUNICATIONS

EXAMPLES

画画	huà huà	to draw; to paint
画家	huà jiā	painter
图画	tú huà	picture

Radical: 田　　Strokes: 8

EXAMPLES

看见	Kàn jiàn	to see; to spot
看书	kàn shū	to read books
看电视	kàn diàn shì	to watch TV

Radical: 目　　Strokes: 9

COMMUNICATIONS

EXAMPLES

问答	wèn dá	questions and answers
问题	wèn tí	question
问候	wèn hòu	greetings

Radical: 门   Strokes: 6

EXAMPLES

很吵	hěn chǎo	very noisy
吵闹	chǎo nào	noisy
吵架	chǎo jià	to quarrel

Radical: 口   Strokes: 7

ACTIONS

zuò
坐
to sit

EXAMPLES

请坐	qǐng zuò	please sit
坐下	zuò xià	to sit down
坐车	zuò chē	take the car or bus

Radical: 土　　Strokes: 7

qǐ
起
to rise

EXAMPLES

起床	qǐ chuáng	to get up (from bed)
起来	qǐ lái	to rise up
起点	qǐ diǎn	starting point

Radical: 走　　Strokes: 10

ACTIONS

kāi 开 — to open; turn on

一 二 テ 开

EXAMPLES

开车	kāi chē	to drive
开门	kāi mén	to open door
开灯	kāi dēng	to turn on light

Radical: 廾   Strokes: 4

guān 关 — to close; turn off

丶 丷 ⺶ 兰 关 关

EXAMPLES

开关	kāi guān	switch
关门	guān mén	close the door
关灯	guān dēng	turn off the light

Radical: 丷   Strokes: 6

ACTIONS

EXAMPLES

进来	jìn lái	to come in
进门	jìn mén	to enter the door
进口	jìn kǒu	to import

Radical: 辶　Strokes: 7

EXAMPLES

出去	chū qù	to get out
出门	chū mén	to go out
出口	chū kǒu	to export; exit

Radical: 凵　Strokes: 5

ACTIONS

zuò 做 — to do

ノ 亻 亻 什 什 估 估 做 做 做

EXAMPLES

做好	zuò hǎo	to do well
做饭	zuò fàn	to cook
做梦	zuò mèng	to dream

Radical: 亻　　Strokes: 11

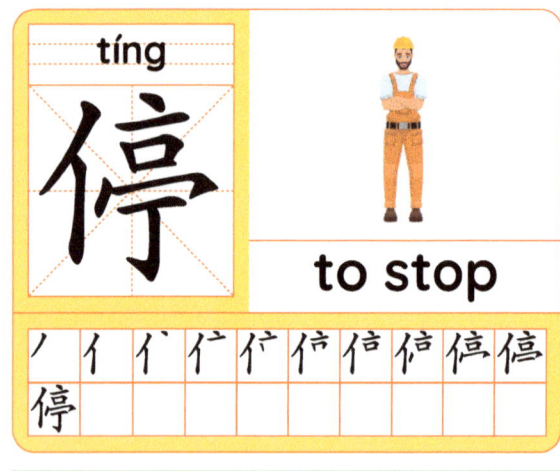

tíng 停 — to stop

ノ 亻 亻 亻 广 广 停 停 信 停

EXAMPLES

停电	tíng diàn	to cut off power
停车	tíng chē	to park the car
停下	tíng xià	to stop

Radical: 亻　　Strokes: 11

ACTIONS

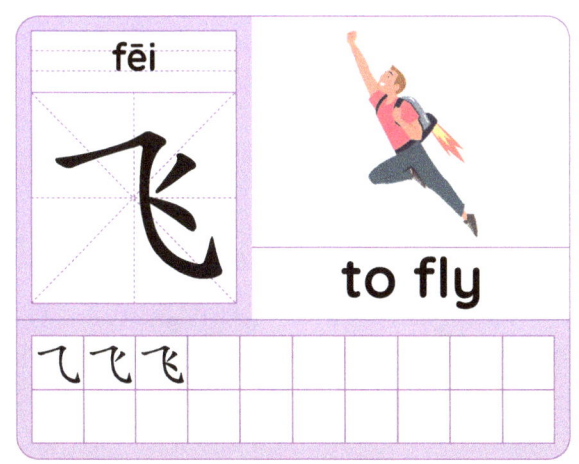

EXAMPLES

飞机	fēi jī	airplane
飞船	fēi chuán	spaceship
起飞	qǐ fēi	to take off

Radical: 飞 Strokes: 3

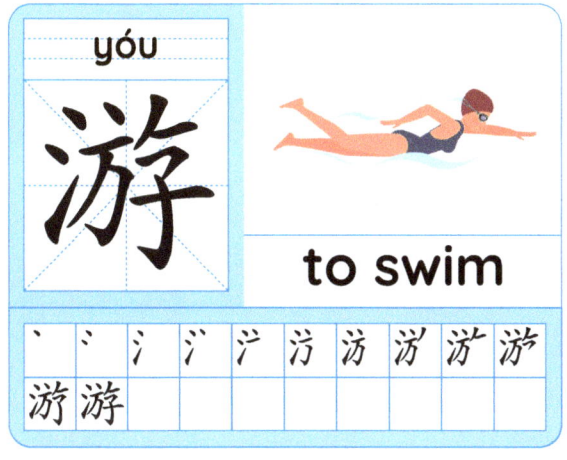

EXAMPLES

游泳	yóu yǒng	to swim
游船	yóu chuán	cruise ship
游客	yóu kè	tourist

Radical: 氵 Strokes: 12

ACTIONS

zǒu — to walk

一 十 土 キ 卡 走 走

EXAMPLES

走路	zǒu lù	to walk
走廊	zǒu láng	aisle
走一走	zǒu yi zǒu	have a walk

Radical: 走   Strokes: 7

pǎo — to run

丶 口 口 甲 早 足 趵 趵 跑 跑

EXAMPLES

跑步	pǎo bù	to run
跑车	pǎo chē	racing car
跑一跑	pǎo yi pǎo	have a run

Radical: 足   Strokes: 12

— 46 —

ACTIONS

dòng 动 to move

一 二 云 云 动 动

EXAMPLES

动作	dòng zuò	action
动物	dòng wù	animal
运动	yùn dòng	sports; exercise

Radical: 力 Strokes: 6

pá 爬 to climb

丿 厂 爫 爫 爫 爫 爬 爬

EXAMPLES

爬树	pá shù	to climb trees
爬山	pá shān	to climb mountains
爬墙	pá qiáng	to climb walls

Radical: 爪 Strokes: 8

ACTIONS

EXAMPLES

唱歌	chàng gē	to sing (songs)
唱片	chàng piàn	musical album
弹唱	tán chàng	to sing and play (music)

Radical: 口   Strokes: 11

EXAMPLES

跳水	tiào shuǐ	to dive
跳伞	tiào sǎn	to skydive
跳舞	tiào wǔ	to dance

Radical: 足   Strokes: 13

ACTIONS

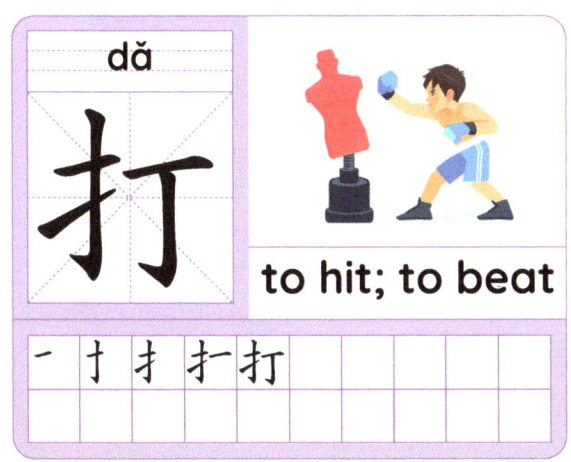

打架	dǎ jià	to fight
打车	dǎ chē	to take a taxi
打电话	dǎ diàn huà	to make phone calls

Radical: 扌   Strokes: 5

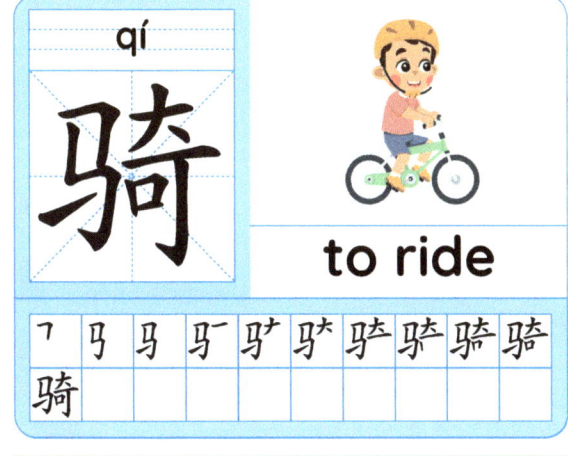

EXAMPLES

骑马	qí mǎ	to ride a horse
骑车	qí chē	to ride a bike
骑士	qí shì	knight

Radical: 马   Strokes: 11

ANIMALS

EXAMPLES

鼠年	shǔ nián	Year of the Rat
老鼠	lǎo shǔ	mouse; rat
鼠标	shǔ biāo	computer mouse

Radical: 鼠   Strokes: 13

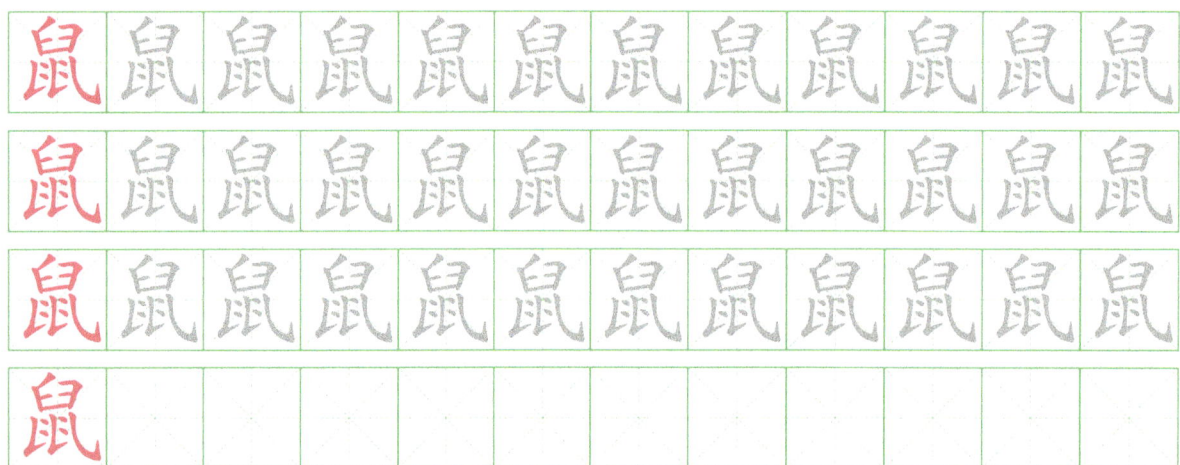

EXAMPLES

牛年	niú nián	Year of the Ox
老牛	lǎo niú	old cow
牛奶	niú nǎi	milk (COW)

Radical: 牛   Strokes: 4

ANIMALS

EXAMPLES

虎年	hǔ nián	Year of the Tiger
老虎	lǎo hǔ	tiger
虎牙	hǔ yá	tiger tooth

Radical: 虍   Strokes: 8

EXAMPLES

兔年	tù nián	Year of the Rabbit
兔子	tù zi	rabbit
属兔	shǔ tù	born in the Year of the Rabbit

Radical: 儿   Strokes: 8

ANIMALS

lóng 龙 — dragon

一 ナ 尤 龙 龙

EXAMPLES

龙年	lóng nián	Year of the Dragon
龙王	lóng wáng	dragon king
龙虾	lóng xiā	lobster

Radical: 龙   Strokes: 5

shé 蛇 — snake

丶 丷 口 中 虫 虫 虫 虫 虫 蚱 蛇 蛇

EXAMPLES

蛇年	shé nián	Year of the Snake
蛇头	shé tóu	snake head
蛇尾	shé wěi	snake tail

Radical: 虫   Strokes: 11

— 52 —

ANIMALS

EXAMPLES		
马年	mǎ nián	Year of the Horse
马路	mǎ lù	road; street
马车	mǎ chē	carriage

Radical: 马 Strokes: 3

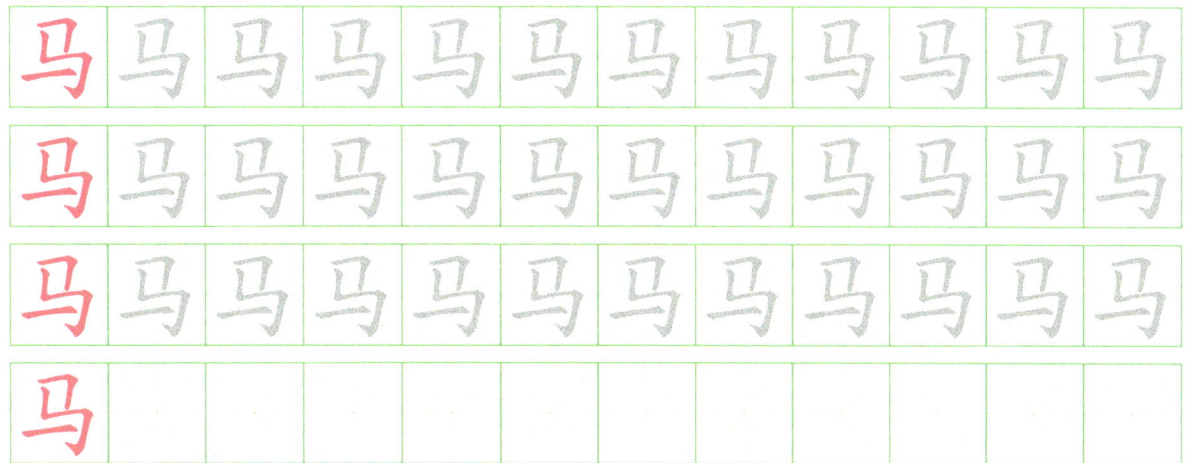

EXAMPLES		
羊年	yáng nián	Year of the Sheep/Goat
山羊	shān yáng	goat
绵羊	mián yáng	sheep

Radical: 羊 Strokes: 6

ANIMALS

hóu — monkey

Strokes: ノ 亻 犭 犭 犴 犴 犼 犼 猴 猴 猴

EXAMPLES

猴年	hóu nián	Year of the Monkey
猴子	hóu zi	monkey
猴王	hóu wáng	monkey king

Radical: 犭   Strokes: 12

jī — chicken; rooster

Strokes: ᄀ ヌ 刄 ヌ′ 鸡 鸡 鸡

EXAMPLES

鸡年	jī nián	Year of the Rooster
鸡肉	jī ròu	chicken
鸡蛋	jī dàn	egg

Radical: 鸟   Strokes: 7

ANIMALS

EXAMPLES

狗年	gǒu nián	Year of the Dog
小狗	xiǎo gǒu	puppy; small dog
属狗	shǔ gǒu	born in the Year of the Dog

Radical: 犭   Strokes: 8

EXAMPLES

猪年	zhū nián	Year of the Pig
猪肉	zhū ròu	pork
猪头	zhū tóu	pig head

Radical: 犭   Strokes: 11

ANIMALS

máo — 猫 — cat

丿 犭 犭 犭 犭 犭 猫 猫 猫

EXAMPLES

公猫	gōng māo	male cat
母猫	mǔ māo	female cat
熊猫	xióng māo	panda

Radical: 犭   Strokes: 11

chóng — 虫 — insect; worm

丨 口 口 中 虫 虫

EXAMPLES

虫子	chóng zi	bug; worm
昆虫	kūn chóng	insect
蚊虫	wén chóng	mosquito

Radical: 虫   Strokes: 6

ANIMALS

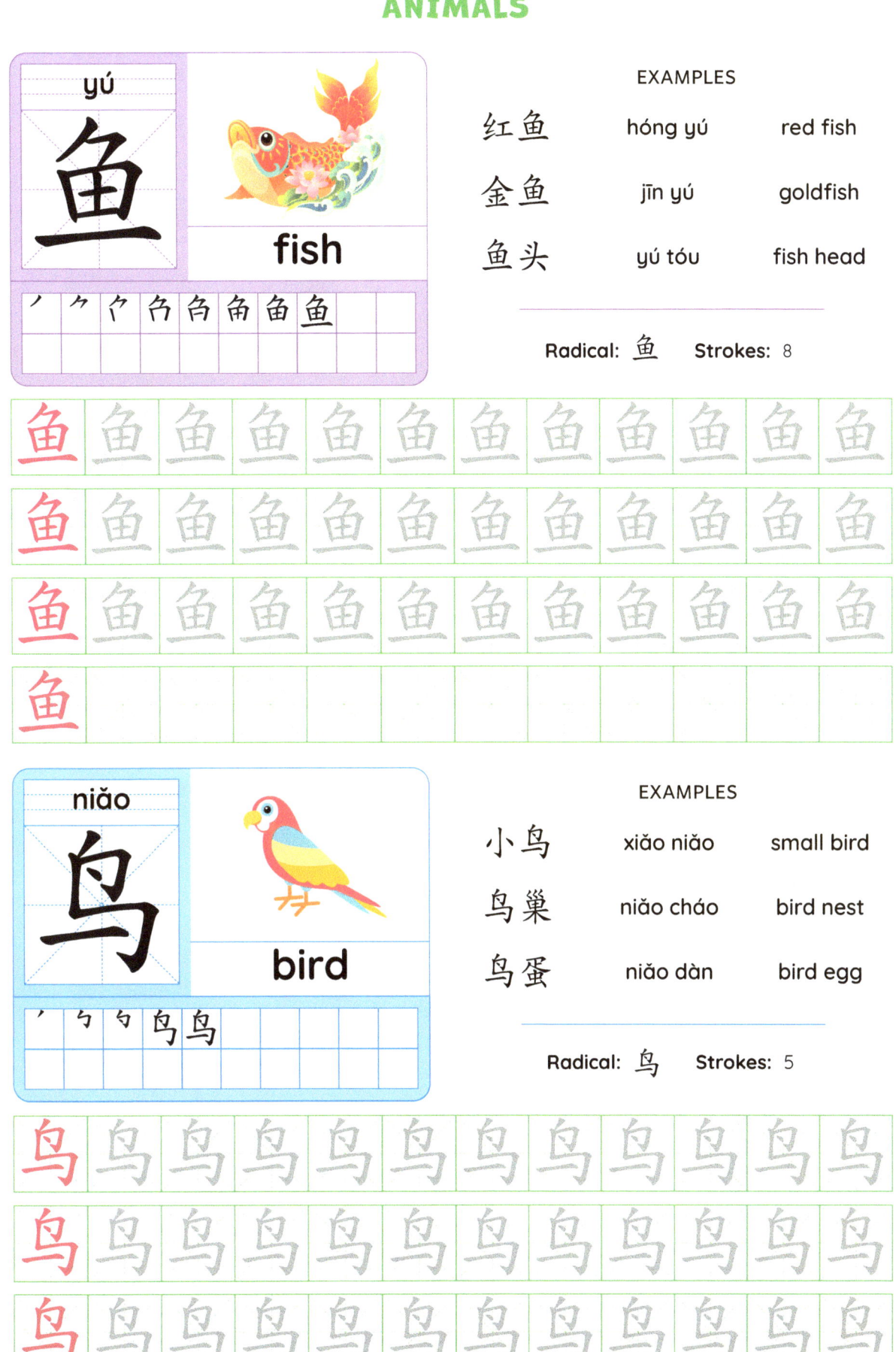

EXAMPLES

红鱼	hóng yú	red fish
金鱼	jīn yú	goldfish
鱼头	yú tóu	fish head

Radical: 鱼   Strokes: 8

EXAMPLES

小鸟	xiǎo niǎo	small bird
鸟巢	niǎo cháo	bird nest
鸟蛋	niǎo dàn	bird egg

Radical: 鸟   Strokes: 5

COLORS

EXAMPLES

红色	hóng sè	red color
红包	hóng bāo	red packet
红酒	hóng jiǔ	red wine

Radical: 纟   Strokes: 6

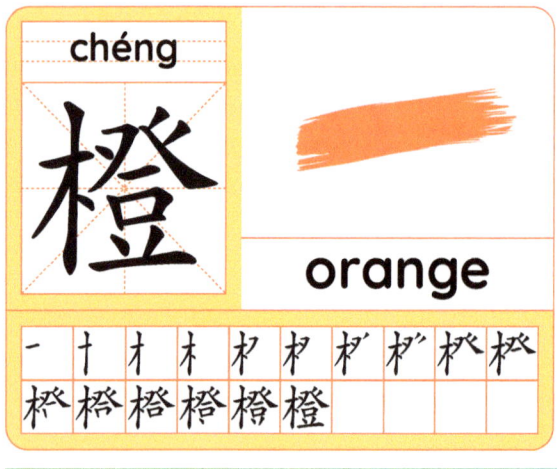

EXAMPLES

橙色	chéng sè	orange color
橙子	chéng zi	orange (fruit)
橙汁	chéng zhī	orange juice

Radical: 木   Strokes: 16

COLORS

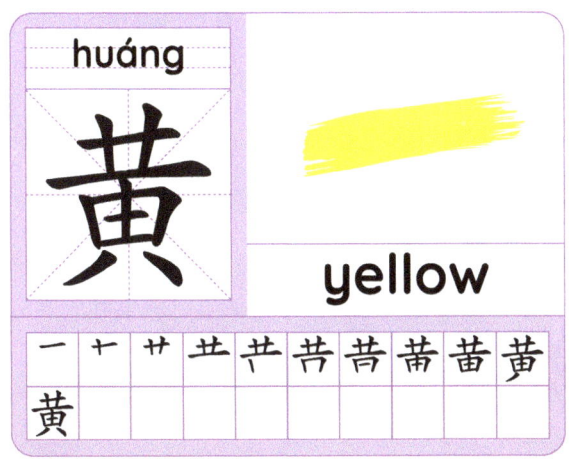

EXAMPLES

黄色　　huáng sè　　yellow color
黄金　　huáng jīn　　gold
黄瓜　　huáng guā　　cucumber

Radical: 黄　　Strokes: 11

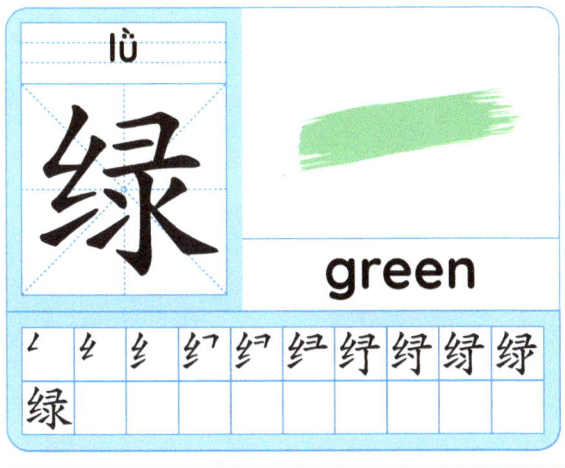

EXAMPLES

绿色　　lǜ sè　　green color
绿豆　　lǜ dòu　　green bean
绿茶　　lǜ chá　　green tea

Radical: 纟　　Strokes: 11

COLORS

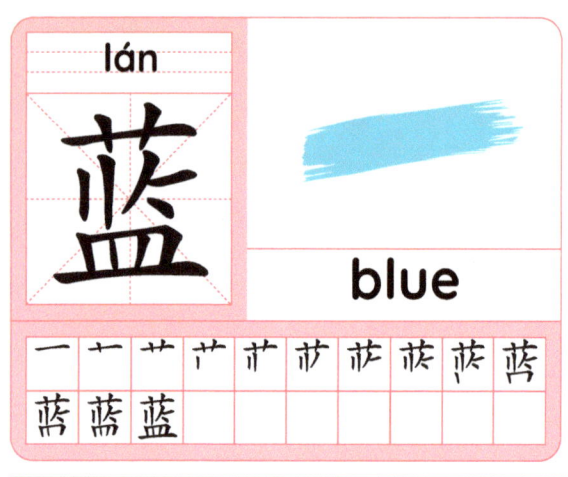

EXAMPLES

蓝色	lán sè	blue color
蓝天	lán tiān	blue sky
蓝牙	lán yá	Bluetooth

Radical: 艹　　Strokes: 13

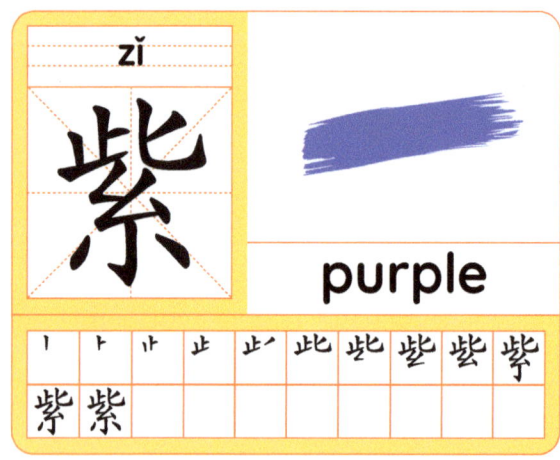

EXAMPLES

紫色	zǐ sè	purple color
深紫	shēn zǐ	dark purple
浅紫	qiǎn zǐ	light purple

Radical: 糸　　Strokes: 12

COLORS

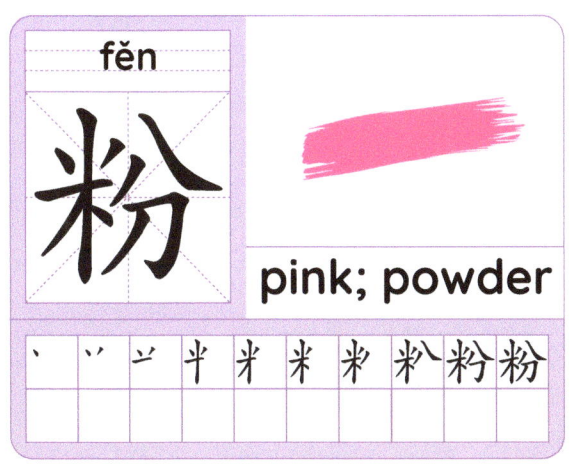

EXAMPLES

粉色	fěn sè	pink color
面粉	miàn fěn	flour
米粉	mǐ fěn	rice noodles

Radical: 米   Strokes: 10

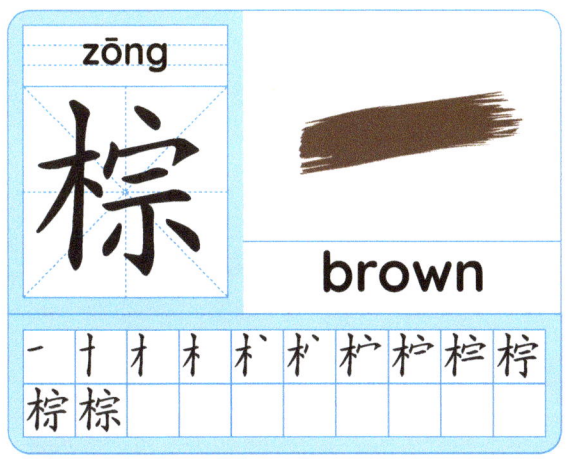

EXAMPLES

棕色	zōng sè	brown color
棕熊	zōng xióng	brown bear
棕灰	zōng huī	brown and gray

Radical: 木   Strokes: 12

COLORS

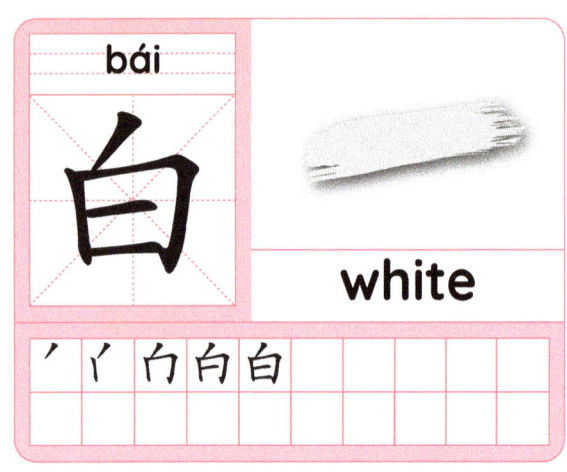

EXAMPLES

白色	bái sè	white color
白天	bái tiān	daytime
白云	bái yún	white cloud

Radical: 白　　Strokes: 5

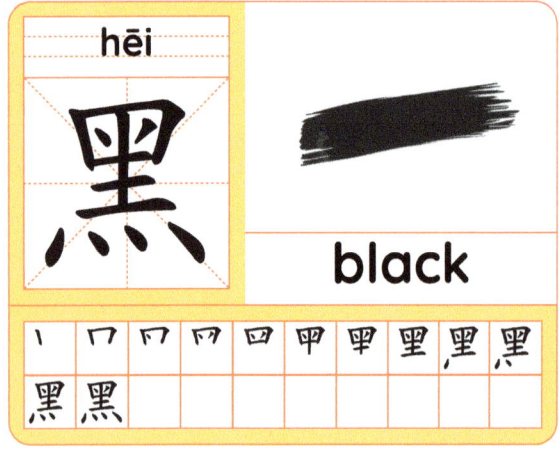

EXAMPLES

黑色	hēi sè	black color
黑夜	hēi yè	dark night
黑暗	hēi àn	darkness

Radical: 灬　　Strokes: 12

FURNITURE

EXAMPLES

桌子	zhuō zi	table
桌布	zhuō bù	tablecloth
桌球	zhuō qiú	Billiards or Pool (a cue sport)

Radical: 木   Strokes: 10

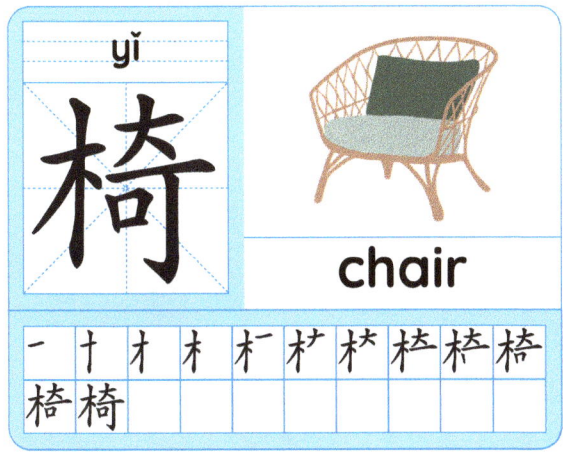

EXAMPLES

椅子	yǐ zi	chair
桌椅	zhuō yǐ	tables and chairs
椅垫	yǐ diàn	chair cushion

Radical: 木   Strokes: 12

FURNITURE

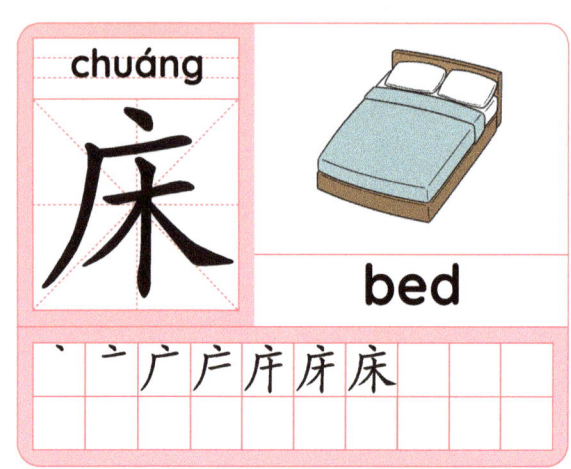

chuáng 床 bed

丶 亠 广 广 庁 庆 床

EXAMPLES

床上　chuáng shàng　on the bed
床下　chuáng xià　under the bed
一张床　yì zhāng chuáng　a bed

Radical: 广　Strokes: 7

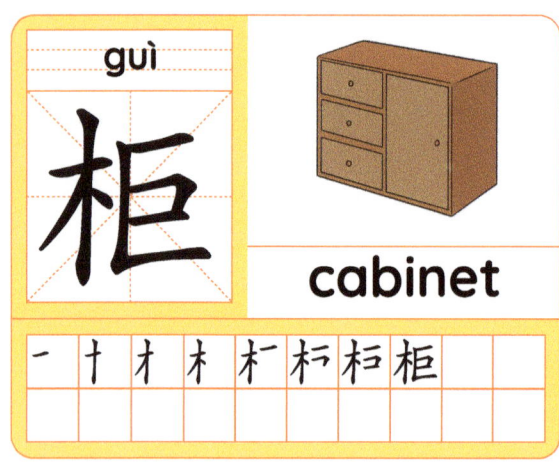

guì 柜 cabinet

一 十 扌 木 朾 柜 柜 柜

EXAMPLES

柜子　guì zi　cabinet
衣柜　yī guì　wardrobe
柜台　guì tái　counter

Radical: 木　Strokes: 8

CONDITION AND APPEARANCE

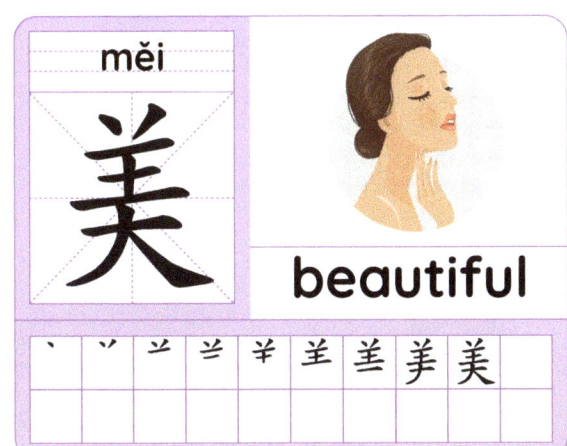

měi 美 beautiful

EXAMPLES
美人	měi rén	beauty
美国	měi guó	America
美食	měi shí	delicious food

Radical: 羊　Strokes: 9

chǒu 丑 ugly

EXAMPLES
丑人	chǒu rén	ugly person
小丑	xiǎo chǒu	clown
很丑	hěn chǒu	very ugly

Radical: 一　Strokes: 4

CONDITION AND APPEARANCE

lǎo
老
old (age)

一 十 土 耂 耂 老

EXAMPLES

老人	lǎo rén	old people
老师	lǎo shī	teacher
老板	lǎo bǎn	boss

Radical: 耂   Strokes: 6

yòu
幼
little (age)

乙 幺 幺 幻 幼

EXAMPLES

幼稚	yòu zhì	childish
幼儿	yòu ér	infant
幼儿园	yòu ér yuán	kindergarten

Radical: 幺   Strokes: 5

CONDITION AND APPEARANCE

EXAMPLES

新书	xīn shū	new book
新年	xīn nián	new year
新房	xīn fáng	new house

Radical: 斤   Strokes: 13

EXAMPLES

旧书	jiù shū	old book
旧版	jiù bǎn	old edition
旧房	jiù fáng	old house

Radical: 日   Strokes: 5

CONDITION AND APPEARANCE

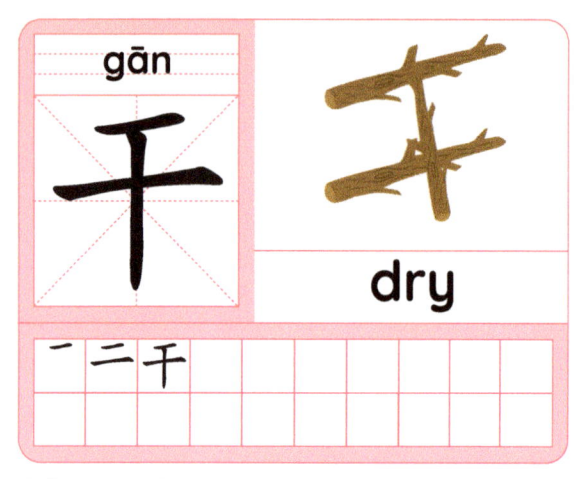

EXAMPLES

干燥	gān zào	dry (weather)
干净	gān jìng	clean
干杯	gān bēi	Cheers (when drinking)

Radical: 干　Strokes: 3

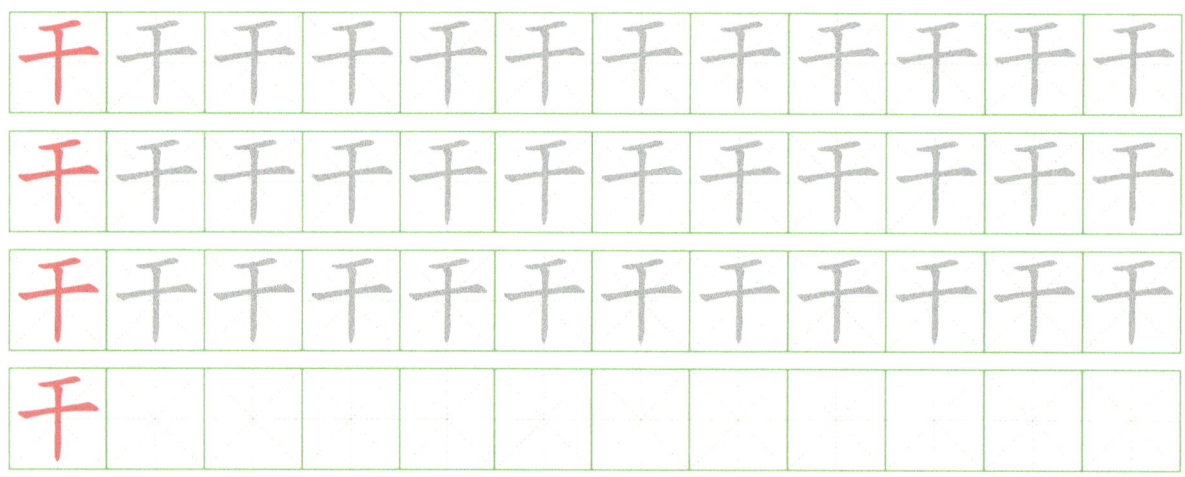

EXAMPLES

湿了	shī le	got wet
湿地	shī dì	wetland
潮湿	cháo shī	humid

Radical: 氵　Strokes: 12

QUALITY AND STATE

EXAMPLES

好人	hǎo rén	good person
好心	hǎo xīn	kind-hearted
好看	hǎo kàn	good looking

Radical: 女   Strokes: 6

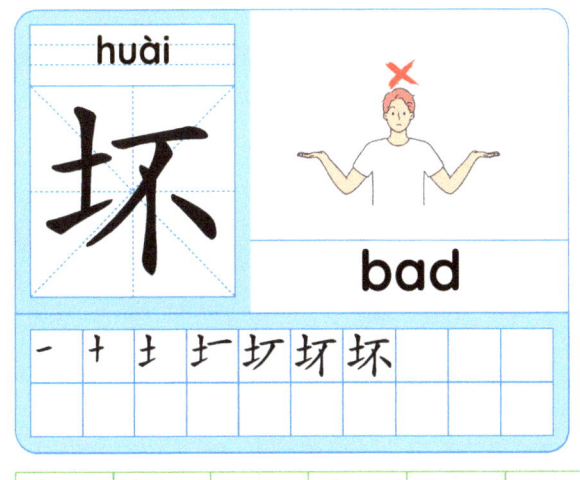

EXAMPLES

坏人	huài rén	bad person
坏蛋	huài dàn	jerk
坏话	huài huà	malicious talk

Radical: 土   Strokes: 7

— 69 —

QUALITY AND STATE

EXAMPLES

快车	kuài chē	express train
快速	kuài sù	fast speed
快点	kuài diǎn	to hurry up

Radical: 忄   Strokes: 7

EXAMPLES

慢车	màn chē	slow train
慢速	màn sù	slow speed
慢点	màn diǎn	to slow down

Radical: 忄   Strokes: 14

— 70 —

QUALITY AND STATE

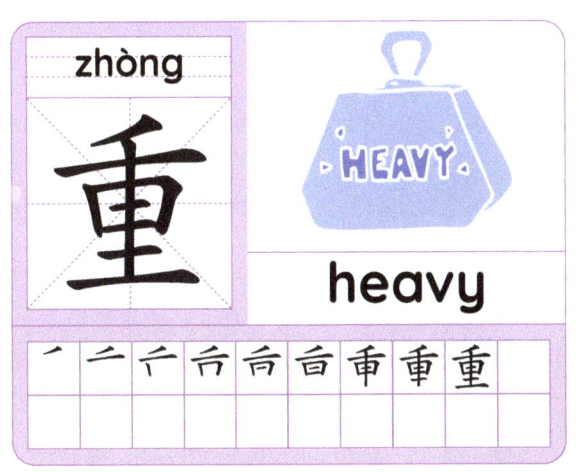

EXAMPLES

重量	zhòng liàng	weight
重要	zhòng yào	important
重点	zhòng diǎn	the key point

Radical: 里   Strokes: 9

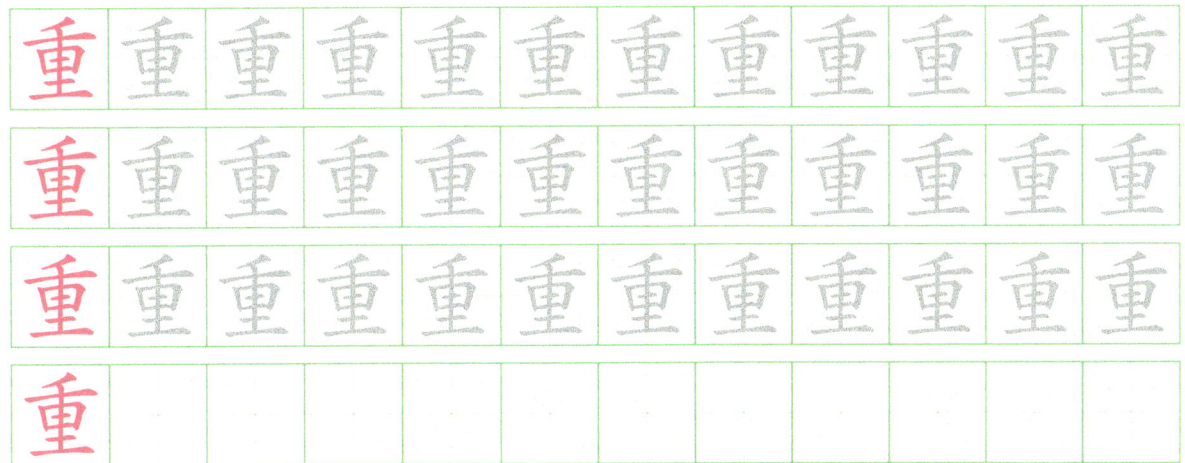

EXAMPLES

年轻	nián qīng	young
轻松	qīng sōng	relaxing
轻点	qīng diǎn	to be gentle

Radical: 车   Strokes: 9

QUALITY AND STATE

EXAMPLES

很香	hěn xiāng	very fragrant
香水	xiāng shuǐ	perfume
香蕉	xiāng jiāo	banana

Radical: 禾   Strokes: 9

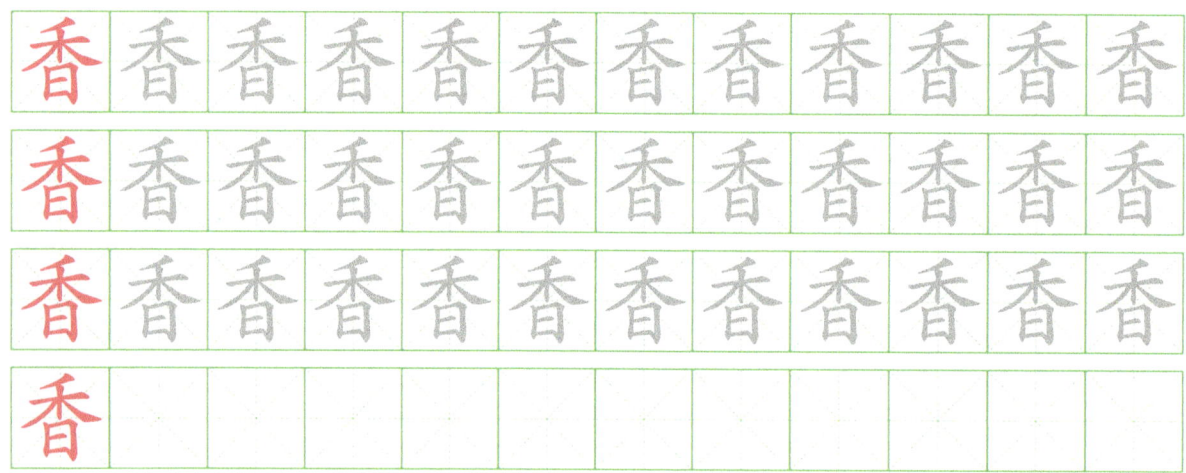

EXAMPLES

很臭	hěn chòu	very smelly
臭虫	chòu chóng	bedbug
臭气	chòu qì	bad smell

Radical: 自   Strokes: 10

QUALITY AND STATE

EXAMPLES

很忙	hěn máng	very busy
不忙	bù máng	not busy
忙人	máng rén	busy person

Radical: 忄　Strokes: 6

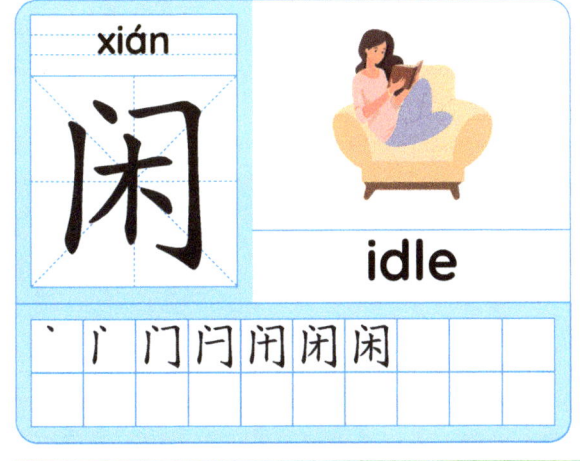

EXAMPLES

很闲	hěn xián	very idle
不闲	bù xián	not idle
闲人	xián rén	idle person

Radical: 门　Strokes: 7

RESOURCES

ACCESS AUDIO

1. Scan the QR code
or go to https://linglingmandarin.com/kidswrite2audio

2. Enter the Book Password: **DOG88**

300 ESSENTIAL CHINESE CHARACTERS WORKBOOK SERIES

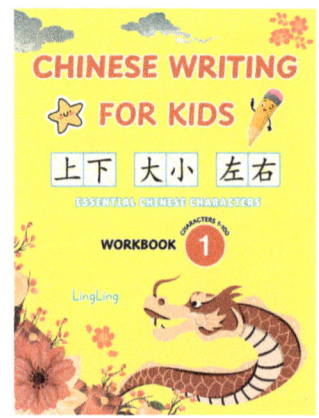  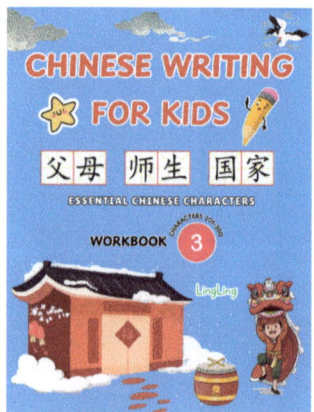

Workbook 1　　　　Workbook 2　　　　Workbook 3
(1 - 100)　　　　　(101 - 200)　　　　(201 - 300)

WRITING PRACTICE BOOKS

BEGINNER BOOKS

LEARN CHINESE VOCABULARY FOR BEGINNERS: NEW HSK 1

CHINESE STORIES FOR LANGUAGE LEARNERS: ELEMENTARY

CHINESE CONVERSATIONS FOR BEGINNERS

LingLing is a native Chinese Mandarin educator with an MA in Communication and Language. Originally from China, now living in the UK, she is the founder of the learning brand LingLing Mandarin, which aims to create the best resources for learners to master the Chinese language and achieve deep insight into Chinese culture in a fun and illuminating way. For more about LingLing and her books, go to www.linglingmandarin.com

www.ingramcontent.com/pod-product-compliance
Lightning Source LLC
Chambersburg PA
CBHW051318110526
44590CB00031B/4392